Carolyn B. Mathis

BULGARIA

TRAVEL GUIDE 2024 REVEALED

The Ultimate Guidebook to Discover Bulgaria's Hidden Treasures and Visit it like a Local

Table of Contents

Introduction

Welcome to Bulgaria

I had the pleasure of visiting Bulgaria on a crisp morning, a country nestled in the heart of the Balkans with a rich history and diverse landscapes. From the moment I arrived in Sofia, the capital city, I was welcomed with open arms and felt right at home. I was amazed by the mix of Roman ruins, Ottoman mosques, and Soviet-era buildings that adorned the city, and the Alexander Nevsky Cathedral with its golden domes was a sight to behold.

My journey then took me to Plovdiv, often called the "*City of Seven Hills*," where I was captivated by the perfectly preserved Roman Amphitheatre and the vibrant street art and eclectic boutiques of the Kapana Creative District. I then ventured to Varna, a coastal gem on the Black Sea, where I spent hours basking in the sun and swimming in the azure waters. The Archaeological Museum revealed a glimpse of Bulgaria's enigmatic past, and the Sea Garden Park provided a serene escape.

No trip to Bulgaria would be complete without a visit to Rila Monastery, a spiritual sanctuary nestled in the Rila Mountains. I was in awe of the intricate frescoes and ancient icons, and the surrounding natural beauty of the Seven Rila Lakes and the majestic Belogradchik Rocks. I then headed to Bansko, a ski resort paradise in the Pirin Mountains, where I explored the mountainous terrain and the charming village of Shiroka Laka.

I was also able to delve into Bulgarian folklore and traditions. In Koprivshtitsa, a living museum of Bulgarian history, I immersed myself in the country's heritage through traditional music, dance, and local crafts. The Bulgarian Rose Valley celebrated the annual Rose Festival, where I joined the jubilant festivities. I also visited Shumen's Monument to 1300 Years of Bulgaria and the Buzludzha Monument, an abandoned UFO-like building atop a mountain.

I savored traditional Bulgarian dishes bursting with flavors, and the country's wine regions introduced me to exquisite local wines. Traveling with children in Bulgaria was an absolute joy, as we explored adventure parks and zoos and I narrated Bulgarian fairytales to their eager ears. The Bulgarian people's warmth and friendliness left a lasting impression, and I was always grateful for their help and love for their country.

My time in Bulgaria was more than just a trip; it was an immersion into a world of wonder, history, and beauty. From the vibrant cities to the tranquil countryside, the ancient ruins to the breathtaking landscapes, Bulgaria had offered me a kaleidoscope of experiences that I will cherish for a lifetime.

Departing Bulgaria, I was certain that this was not a goodbye, but a pledge to come back. For this concealed gem in the core of the Balkans had become a piece of me, and I realized that eventually, I would find myself once more in its inviting hug.

Bulgaria had not just been a spot; it had become a treasured memory, a place where I had encountered the enchantment of travel and found the abundance of a nation that would always have a unique spot in my heart.

History and Culture

Nestled at the crossroads of Europe and Asia, Bulgaria is a land with a long and fascinating history. Its unique identity has been shaped by ancient civilizations, fierce battles, and thriving arts and traditions.

The Thracians were the first to inhabit Bulgaria, leaving behind exquisite gold and silver artifacts, burial mounds, and rock sanctuaries, such as the Thracian Tomb of Kazanlak, which is now a UNESCO World Heritage Site. When the Roman Empire conquered Bulgaria in the 1st century AD, it brought with it Roman architecture, engineering, and the Latin language. Later, during the Byzantine Empire, Bulgaria became a center of Orthodox Christianity.

In the 7th century, the Bulgarians established their first state, known as the First Bulgarian Empire. Its capital, Pliska, was a bustling cultural and political center, and during this time, Cyrillic script, the basis of the modern Bulgarian alphabet, was created by Saint Cyril and Saint Methodius. The First Bulgarian Empire experienced a

Golden Age during the reign of Tsar Simeon I (893-927 AD).

In 1396, Bulgaria fell under Ottoman rule, a period of suppression and hardship for the Bulgarian people. However, the spirit of the nation remained resilient, and the National Revival period emerged in the 18th and 19th centuries. This era saw a cultural awakening, with a renewed interest in its history, language, and traditions. In 1878, Bulgaria achieved its independence and emerged as a modern nation.

The 20th century brought challenges, particularly during the World Wars. After the war, Bulgaria fell under communist rule, and the Bulgarian Communist Party established a one-party state with tight control over all aspects of life. In 1989, the fall of the Berlin Wall marked the beginning of significant changes in Bulgaria, leading to the end of communist rule in 1990. Bulgaria embraced economic reforms and became a member of the European Union in 2007.

Bulgaria's culture is a vibrant tapestry of its diverse history and traditions. Its folk music and dance are an integral part of its identity, and the unique polyphonic singing, called

"Bulgarian throat singing," is renowned for its beauty. Traditional Bulgarian cuisine is a delightful fusion of flavors, from the famous Bulgarian yogurt to the mouthwatering banitsa (cheese-filled pastry) and Shopska salad. Religion plays a significant role in Bulgarian culture, with the Eastern Orthodox Church being the dominant faith.

Bulgarians are renowned for their hospitality and friendliness, making visitors feel welcome and appreciated. Art and craftsmanship have also been a part of Bulgaria's history, with skilled artisans creating beautiful pottery, woodcarvings, and traditional costumes that reflect the cultural identity of the different regions. Festivals and celebrations are an important part of Bulgarian culture, with events such as Kukeri (a traditional masked dance) and Baba Marta (celebrating the arrival of spring) being popular among both locals and tourists.

Geography and Climate

Bulgaria is a stunning country located in Southeast Europe, bordered by Romania to the north, Serbia and North Macedonia to the west, Greece and Turkey to the south, and the Black Sea to the east. It is a true jewel of the Balkans, boasting a variety of landscapes and ecosystems that captivate visitors from all over the world.

The Balkan Mountains, also known as Stara Planina, run from the western border to the eastern part of the country and are a defining feature of Bulgaria's geography. These majestic mountains serve as a natural divide between northern and southern Bulgaria, with deep gorges and fertile valleys nestled between its peaks.

In the southwestern part of the country, the Rila and Pirin Mountains offer some of the highest peaks in the Balkans, with Mount Musala standing at 2,925 meters (9,596 feet). These mountain ranges are home to beautiful glacial lakes, lush alpine meadows, and dense forests, making them a paradise for hikers and nature enthusiasts.

The Rhodope Mountains, which stretch across the southern part of Bulgaria and into Greece, are a picturesque blend of rolling hills, rocky formations, and deep river valleys. This region is famous for its rich folklore and mythology, adding an air of enchantment to its already captivating scenery.

The northern part of Bulgaria is dominated by the vast Danube Plain, a fertile and agriculturally significant region. The Danube River, one of Europe's major waterways, flows along the northern border, creating a natural boundary with Romania. The fertile plains alongside the river are ideal for agriculture and are a vital part of Bulgaria's economy.

The Thracian Plain, situated between the Balkan Mountains to the north and the Sredna Gora Mountains to the south, is another essential geographical region of Bulgaria. This fertile plain is rich in agriculture and is home to some of the country's most historically significant cities, including Plovdiv, one of the oldest continually inhabited cities in Europe.

The eastern border of Bulgaria is blessed with a breathtaking coastline along the Black Sea. The Bulgarian Black Sea Coast stretches for over 350 kilometers (217 miles) and boasts picturesque sandy beaches, charming coastal towns, and vibrant seaside resorts such as Sunny Beach and Golden Sands. This region is a popular tourist destination during the summer months, attracting visitors from all over Europe seeking sun, sea, and relaxation.

Bulgaria's climate is quite diverse due to its varying geography. The northern and central parts of the country have a continental climate with cold winters and hot summers, while the southern coastal region along the Black Sea enjoys a Mediterranean climate with mild winters and warm summers. The high mountain ranges of Rila and Pirin experience an alpine climate with cold winters and mild summers, and the southern part of Bulgaria, including the Thracian Plain and the Rhodope Mountains, falls under a sub-Mediterranean climate with milder winters and pleasantly warm summers.

Planning Your Trip

Best Time to Visit Bulgaria

Bulgaria, a captivating country situated in the Balkans, offers a wide range of experiences to travelers all year round. From its stunning Black Sea coastline to its picturesque mountains and vibrant cities, each season brings its own unique charm to this bewitching destination. Deciding the best time to visit Bulgaria depends on your preferences, whether you are looking for sunny beach days, winter sports, cultural festivals, or tranquil nature retreats. Let's explore each season and find out the optimal time to embark on your Bulgarian journey.

Spring (March to May):

Spring is a great time to visit Bulgaria, as the country comes out of its winter hibernation. The landscape is adorned with vibrant blooms, and nature is alive with fresh greenery. In March, the ski resorts still offer great conditions for winter sports fans, while the warmer temperatures make outdoor activities more enjoyable. The

Rhodope Mountains and Rila Mountains are ideal for spring hikes amidst stunning scenery. Don't miss the magnificent Rila Monastery, where the surrounding natural beauty is at its peak during this season.

Spring in Bulgaria is also associated with cultural festivities. On March 1st, Bulgarians celebrate Baba Marta, a tradition involving the exchange of Martenitsi (red and white tassels) symbolizing the arrival of spring. Plovdiv, the European Capital of Culture, hosts various art and music festivals during this time, making it a cultural paradise for visitors.

Summer (June to August):

Summer is undoubtedly the peak season for tourism in Bulgaria, and for good reason. The coastal towns of Varna, Golden Sands, and Sunny Beach come alive with sunseekers, water sports lovers, and beachgoers. The Black Sea's inviting waters are perfect for swimming and leisurely beach days. Along the Bulgarian Riviera, you'll find a wealth of beachfront resorts, lively nightlife, and beachfront promenades bustling with activity.

Venturing inland, the lush landscapes of the Balkan Mountains and the sunny plains offer ideal conditions for hiking, picnics, and exploring quaint villages. Bulgaria's cities, including Sofia, Plovdiv, and Veliko Tarnovo, boast pleasant weather, allowing visitors to explore their historical sites and cultural attractions comfortably.

If you are a music enthusiast, don't miss the vibrant festivals and open-air concerts taking place during the summer months. From the Burgas Music Festival to the Varna Summer International Music Festival, Bulgaria's summer events calendar is filled with captivating performances.

Autumn (September to November):

Autumn casts a spell of enchantment on Bulgaria, as the country's landscapes transform into a stunning tapestry of autumn colors. The weather remains pleasant, making it an ideal time for exploring the country's natural wonders, such as the Seven Rila Lakes and the Belogradchik Rocks. The picturesque vineyards in the Melnik region are especially charming during this season, offering wine lovers a delightful experience.

September and October bring the harvest season, which is celebrated with numerous festivals across the country. The Rose Festival in Kazanlak is a highlight, where visitors can witness the centuries-old tradition of rose oil production and indulge in the festivities.

For history buffs, autumn is a great time to explore Bulgaria's ancient sites, including the Thracian tombs and the Roman ruins in Plovdiv and Nessebar. The cooler temperatures also make city sightseeing more comfortable.

Winter (December to February):

Winter in Bulgaria offers a magical escape for snow lovers and winter sports fans. The ski resorts of Bansko, Borovets, and Pamporovo come alive with skiers and snowboarders, offering excellent conditions for winter activities. The Pirin and Rila Mountains are adorned with glistening snow, creating a picturesque winter wonderland.

For those seeking a more serene winter retreat, the charming villages in the Rhodope Mountains offer a peaceful ambiance and the opportunity to experience traditional Bulgarian culture and hospitality. Cozy up in a traditional guesthouse and savor delicious homemade dishes.

During the winter months, Bulgaria's cities are adorned with festive lights and decorations, creating a joyful atmosphere. Sofia's Christmas Market and New Year celebrations are not to be missed, providing a warm and festive welcome to the new year.

Visa and Entry Requirements

Bulgaria is a destination that captivates the hearts of travelers from all over the world with its rich history, stunning landscapes, and vibrant culture. If you're planning a trip to Bulgaria, it's important to understand the visa and entry requirements to ensure a smooth and hassle-free journey. In this section, we'll cover the various visa types, entry regulations, and important travel considerations to help you make the most of your time in this enchanting Balkan nation.

For many travelers, the good news is that Bulgaria allows visa-free entry for citizens of several countries. As of September 2021, citizens of the European Union (EU) member states, the European Economic Area (EEA), and Switzerland can enter Bulgaria without a visa and stay for up to 90 days within a 180-day period. Additionally, citizens of non-EU countries like the United States, Canada, Australia, New Zealand, Japan, South Korea, and many others can also enjoy visa-free entry for up to 90 days within a 180-day period.

If you hold a valid Schengen visa, you can enter Bulgaria without the need for an additional Bulgarian visa. This applies to travelers who plan to visit Bulgaria for up to 90 days within a 180-day period. However, it's important to check if your Schengen visa allows for multiple entries, as single-entry visas may restrict re-entry to Bulgaria after leaving the country.

For travelers intending to stay in Bulgaria for more than 90 days, a long-stay visa, also known as a Type D visa, is required. This visa is suitable for various purposes, including work, study, family reunification, or long-term residence. To obtain a Type D visa, you must apply at the Bulgarian embassy or consulate in your home country before your departure. The application process may involve submitting supporting documents, such as a letter of invitation, employment contract, proof of accommodation, and proof of sufficient funds to cover your stay.

When applying for a Bulgarian visa, you will typically need to provide a valid passport with a minimum validity of six months beyond your intended stay in Bulgaria, a completed visa application form, recent passport-sized photos, proof of travel insurance, proof of accommodation, evidence of sufficient financial means, and a round-trip flight itinerary or travel reservations. The processing time for Bulgarian visa applications may vary depending on the embassy or consulate where you apply, so it's best to apply well in advance of your planned travel dates.

If you find yourself in Bulgaria and wish to extend your stay beyond the authorized period, you must apply for an extension at the Migration Directorate of the Ministry of Interior. Extension requests are usually granted for valid reasons, such as medical treatment, family emergencies, or other unforeseen circumstances. It is essential to initiate the extension process before your current visa expires to avoid any potential penalties or visa violations.

Overstaying your visa in Bulgaria is taken seriously and can lead to fines, deportation, or entry bans for future visits. If you have any uncertainties or encounter unexpected situations, contact the local Migration Directorate or the nearest embassy or consulate for guidance and assistance. In the event of any emergencies, lost or stolen passports, or legal issues during your stay in Bulgaria, your country's embassy or consulate can provide consular assistance. It's wise to register your trip with your embassy or consulate before traveling, enabling them to assist you better in case of any unforeseen circumstances.

When visiting Bulgaria, it is important to be aware of the local laws, customs, and traditions. Bulgarians are known for their hospitality, so it is essential to be respectful of cultural differences and act accordingly. When visiting religious sites, dress modestly and avoid any illegal or disrespectful activities.

Transportation in Bulgaria

To make the most of your journey, it's important to understand the transportation system and the various options available. Whether you're visiting the historic streets of Sofia, exploring the countryside, or heading to the Black Sea coast, Bulgaria has something to offer every traveler.

In the cities, buses are a popular and cost-effective way to get around. Sofia, Plovdiv, Varna, and Burgas all have well-developed bus networks that connect different neighborhoods and attractions. Trams and trolleys are also available in Sofia and Plovdiv, providing a scenic ride through the city. For those looking for a quicker journey, Sofia has a modern and efficient metro system.

Inter-city buses are a great way to travel between cities in Bulgaria. Companies like Union Ivkoni, Biomet, and Karat-S offer regular services connecting major cities and towns. The buses are comfortable and equipped with amenities like air conditioning and Wi-Fi. Trains are also a great option for exploring the country's various regions, offering a scenic journey through the picturesque countryside.

For those seeking flexibility and independence, renting a car is a great option. International car rental companies have branches in major Bulgarian cities, offering a wide range of vehicles. Exploring Bulgaria by car allows you to venture off the beaten path and discover hidden gems. Domestic flights are also available, with Bulgaria Air offering flights between Sofia and Varna, Sofia and Burgas, and Sofia and Plovdiv.

Taxis are a common sight in Bulgarian cities and offer a convenient way to get around. Shared rides, or "marshrutkas," are also popular for shorter trips between towns and villages. For those exploring the Black Sea coast, ferries are available to connect certain towns and islands.

Transportation in Bulgaria is generally reliable, affordable, and safe. To ensure a smooth experience, it's important to plan ahead, research the transportation options available, and check schedules, especially in rural areas where services may be less frequent.

Exploring Bulgaria's stunning beauty and unique culture is an unforgettable experience. To make your journey smoother, it's important to understand the country's transportation options and follow some travel tips. When using public transport, make sure to validate your ticket before boarding or entering a train or bus.

Ticket inspectors are common, and fines for not having a valid ticket can be hefty. When taking taxis or shared rides, it's essential to negotiate the fare beforehand to avoid being overcharged. Taxis with meters are usually more reliable.

English is spoken in tourist areas and by younger generations, but it's still helpful to learn a few basic

Bulgarian phrases, especially when visiting smaller towns and rural areas.

Lastly, keep your belongings secure, especially in crowded areas or on public transportation. Petty theft can occur, so stay alert and aware of your surroundings. With these tips in mind, you can explore Bulgaria with ease and create wonderful memories that will last a lifetime.

Accommodation Options

Bulgaria has a wide range of accommodation options, so no matter what your budget or preferences are, you can find a place to stay that suits you. Whether you're looking for a luxurious and pampering experience or a cozy and affordable retreat, the hotels in Bulgaria will make your visit unforgettable. Here are twenty (20) luxurious and affordable hotels you can stay in Bulgaria;

Luxurious Hotels:

1. Arena di Serdica Hotel, Sofia:

This five-star hotel in the heart of Sofia is the perfect blend of modern luxury and historical significance. Built on top of ancient Roman ruins, the Arena di Serdica Hotel offers elegant rooms, a spa center, and a rooftop restaurant with stunning views of the city.

2. Sense Hotel Sofia:

Sense Hotel Sofia is a contemporary hotel set against the backdrop of Vitosha Mountain. It features stylish rooms, an upscale restaurant, a rooftop bar, and a luxurious spa for ultimate relaxation.

3. Grand Hotel Sofia:

The Grand Hotel Sofia is a five-star landmark in Sofia, renowned for its timeless elegance and prime location near the city's main attractions. Guests can enjoy the hotel's spa, rooftop terrace, and gourmet restaurants.

4. Kempinski Hotel Grand Arena, Bansko:

This award-winning ski resort in Bansko offers a luxurious mountain retreat. Kempinski Hotel Grand Arena features spacious rooms, an extensive spa, multiple dining options, and direct access to the ski slopes.

5. Premier Luxury Mountain Resort, Bansko:

For a boutique mountain experience, the Premier Luxury Mountain Resort is a top choice. This five-star hotel offers stylish rooms, an exquisite spa, and a heated outdoor pool with stunning mountain views.

6. BlackSeaRama Golf & Villas, Balchik:

Perched on a cliff overlooking the Black Sea, this luxury resort in Balchik is a golfer's paradise. The BlackSeaRama offers elegant villas, a signature golf course, and a private beach for a serene coastal escape.

7. International Hotel Casino & Tower Suites, Golden Sands:

Set along the famous Golden Sands Beach, this five-star hotel features opulent suites, a lavish casino, an infinity pool, and direct beach access, promising an indulgent seaside vacation.

8. Palace Marina Dinevi Hotel, Sveti Vlas:

Located in the upscale Marina Dinevi complex, this boutique hotel offers stylish rooms with sea views, an elegant restaurant, and access to a private marina and beach.

9. Sunset Resort, Pomorie:

Sunset Resort in Pomorie offers luxurious apartments and a plethora of amenities, including outdoor pools, spa facilities, and a variety of dining options, all set against a contemporary design and beachfront location.

10. Meliá Grand Hermitage, Golden Sands:

An all-inclusive beachfront resort, Meliá Grand Hermitage caters to both families and couples. It boasts spacious rooms, multiple pools, an extensive spa, and an array of dining choices.

11. Santa Marina Holiday Village, Sozopol:

Santa Marina Holiday Village is nestled amidst lush greenery and overlooking the Black Sea. It offers luxurious villas and apartments, a private beach, and a range of recreational activities.

12. Aqua Paradise Resort, Nesebar:

Aqua Paradise Resort is a water park hotel in Nesebar that is perfect for families. It features spacious rooms, numerous water attractions, and easy access to Nesebar's historic Old Town.

AFFORDABLE HOTELS

1. Hotel Downtown, Sofia:

Hotel Downtown is centrally located and offers budget-friendly rooms with modern amenities. Its convenient location makes it ideal for exploring Sofia's main attractions.

2. Art Hostel and B&B, Sofia:

Art Hostel and B&B is a charming and artistic hostel in Sofia that provides budget-conscious travelers with cozy dormitories and private rooms, all decorated with local artwork.

3. Trinity Rocks Farm, Veliko Tarnovo:

Trinity Rocks Farm in Veliko Tarnovo offers affordable rooms in a traditional Bulgarian house, surrounded by nature, for a unique countryside experience.

4. Family Hotel Belvedere, Plovdiv:

Family Hotel Belvedere is located near Plovdiv's Old Town and offers comfortable rooms at a reasonable price, along with beautiful views of the city.

5. Hotel Elegance, Plovdiv:

Hotel Elegance boasts a central location, budget-friendly rooms, and a friendly atmosphere, making it a popular choice for travelers exploring Plovdiv.

6. Hotel Favorit, Varna:

Just a few steps away from Varna's main attractions, Hotel Favorit offers budget-friendly rooms and a rooftop terrace with stunning city views.

7. Hotel mOdus, Varna:

Right in the center of Varna, Hotel mOdus provides stylish and reasonably priced rooms, perfect for travelers who want a touch of luxury without breaking the bank.

l

8. Hotel Bonita, Burgas:

Close to the sea garden and the beach, Hotel Bonita offers comfortable rooms and a friendly atmosphere, making it a great choice for a budget stay in Burgas.

9. Family Hotel Silver Pearl, Sunny Beach:

A short stroll from the vibrant Sunny Beach, Family Hotel Silver Pearl provides affordable rooms and a swimming pool for a peaceful stay.

10. Hotel Strimon Bed & Breakfast, Kyustendil:

Situated in the picturesque town of Kyustendil, Hotel Strimon Bed & Breakfast offers comfortable rooms with mountain views at a budget-friendly price.

11. Family Hotel Gallery, Nesebar:

A family-run hotel in the heart of Nesebar's Old Town, Family Hotel Gallery provides affordable rooms with a charming atmosphere.

12. Hotel Fenerite, Bansko:

In the center of Bansko, Hotel Fenerite offers cozy rooms at an affordable rate, as well as easy access to the ski slopes and town center.

Safety Tips for Travelers

With its rich history, stunning landscapes, and hospitable people, it's a great place to visit. However, like any other country, it's important to be mindful of safety and take certain precautions to ensure a smooth and enjoyable trip. Here are some tips to keep in mind when traveling in Bulgaria:

Be Alert in Busy Areas:

Bulgaria's popular tourist attractions, markets, and public transportation hubs can get crowded, especially during peak seasons. Be aware of your surroundings and keep a close eye on your belongings to avoid pickpocketing. Consider using a secure crossbody bag or a money belt to carry your valuables, and don't carry large amounts of cash.

Use Official Transportation:

When taking taxis or shared rides, always use official and licensed services. Make sure to agree on a fare before starting the journey to avoid any potential misunderstandings. If you're unsure about the legitimacy of a taxi or ride service, ask your accommodation for recommendations or use reputable ride-sharing apps.

Be Cautious at Night:

While Bulgaria is generally safe, it's best to avoid walking alone in unlit and isolated areas at night, especially in unfamiliar neighborhoods. Stick to well-lit streets and main thoroughfares, and consider taking a taxi or using public transportation to get to your destination safely.

Be Wary of Stray Animals:

Bulgaria has its share of stray animals, especially in urban areas. While many of these animals are friendly, it's essential to exercise caution, especially if you encounter a stray dog that seems aggressive or threatened. Avoid approaching them and maintain a safe distance.

Respect Local Customs:

Bulgarians take pride in their customs and traditions, and as a visitor, it's essential to respect their cultural norms. Dress modestly when visiting religious sites, and ask for permission before taking photos of locals or their property. Demonstrating cultural sensitivity will enhance your interactions and leave a positive impression.

Book Accommodations and Transportation in Advance:

To ensure a smooth and stress-free trip, book your accommodations and transportation in advance, especially during peak tourist seasons. Having confirmed reservations will save you the hassle of searching for last-minute options and will provide you with peace of mind during your travels.

Know Emergency Contacts:

Before traveling to Bulgaria, familiarize yourself with emergency contact numbers such as the police (166), ambulance (150), and fire brigade (160). In case of an emergency, knowing these numbers can be crucial for seeking assistance quickly.

Stay Hydrated and Sun-Safe:

During the summer months, Bulgaria can experience high temperatures, especially in coastal areas. Stay hydrated by drinking plenty of water and avoid direct sunlight during peak hours. Consider wearing sunscreen, a wide-brimmed hat, and sunglasses to protect yourself from the sun's rays.

Stay Informed:

Keep yourself updated about local news and events, especially if you plan to attend festivals, demonstrations, or public gatherings. Being informed about any potential safety concerns or disruptions can help you make informed decisions during your travels.

Trust Your Instincts:

Lastly, trust your instincts while traveling in Bulgaria. If something feels off or uncomfortable, remove yourself from the situation. It's always better to err on the side of caution and prioritize your safety.

These safety tips are essential for any traveler, but it's important to remember that Bulgaria is a generally safe country with friendly and welcoming locals. By exercising basic caution and respect, you'll be able to fully embrace the beauty and charm of this Balkan gem, creating cherished memories that will last a lifetime.

Packing Tips and What to Bring

When packing for Bulgaria, it's important to strike a balance between practicality and preparation for the various weather conditions. With these packing tips and a well-organized travel checklist, you'll be ready to make the most of your trip. Whether you're exploring historic cities, venturing into the majestic mountains, or relaxing on the Black Sea coast, here are some tips and a comprehensive list of what to bring.

First, consider the season. Bulgaria has four distinct seasons, each with its own charm. When packing, make sure to take the time of year into account. Spring (March to May) is a lovely time to visit, with mild temperatures and blossoming flowers. Pack light layers, a jacket or sweater, and comfortable walking shoes. Summer (June to August) can get hot, especially in the lowlands and along the coast. Bring lightweight and breathable clothing, such as shorts, t-shirts, and sundresses, as well as a hat, sunglasses, sunscreen, and swimwear. Autumn (September to

November) offers pleasant weather and beautiful foliage. Pack a mix of light and warm clothing, as temperatures can vary throughout the day. Winter (December to February) can be cold, especially in the mountains. Bring warm layers, including thermal clothing, sweaters, and a heavy coat, as well as gloves, a hat, and a scarf.

Comfortable footwear is essential for exploring Bulgaria on foot. Pack a sturdy pair of walking shoes or hiking boots, as well as comfortable sneakers or sandals for city explorations. Don't forget to make sure you have all your travel documents in order, including your passport (with at least six months' validity), travel insurance, flight tickets, and any necessary visas. Pack the appropriate electrical adapters for your devices, as well as chargers for phones, cameras, and other electronics. If you take any prescription medications, make sure to bring an ample supply for your entire trip. Additionally, it's advisable to pack a basic first aid kit with band-aids, pain relievers, antiseptic cream, and any personal medications you may need.

Bulgaria's currency is the Bulgarian Lev (BGN). While credit cards are widely accepted in major cities and tourist areas, it's a good idea to carry some cash, especially for smaller purchases and when visiting rural regions. ATMs are readily available in cities, but they may be less frequent in remote areas.

A comfortable and practical travel backpack or daypack is essential for carrying your essentials while exploring Bulgaria. Choose one with multiple compartments for easy organization. Bring a travel guide or download a travel app that includes maps and useful information about Bulgaria's attractions, restaurants, and cultural sites.

Sun protection is also important, so pack sunscreen with a high SPF, a wide-brimmed hat, and UV-blocking sunglasses. If you're visiting during the summer, don't forget to pack swimwear and beach essentials, including a beach towel, flip-flops, and a beach bag.

If you plan to explore Bulgaria's natural wonders, such as the Seven Rila Lakes or the Black Sea coast, consider bringing waterproof gear, such as a rain jacket or poncho. Additionally, a language guidebook or some basic Bulgarian phrases will be appreciated by locals and enhance your travel experience.

Camera and Binoculars:

Capture the stunning views and wildlife of Bulgaria with a camera or smartphone. If you're a birdwatcher or nature lover, binoculars will make your wildlife viewing experiences even more enjoyable.

Travel Journal and Pen:

Bring a travel journal to document your Bulgarian journey. Don't forget to pack a pen to jot down memories and details that you don't want to forget.

Respectful Attire:

Bulgaria is quite liberal when it comes to clothing, but it's important to dress respectfully when visiting religious sites or rural areas. Some religious sites may require visitors to cover their shoulders and knees.

Snacks and Water:

Bring some snacks and a bottle of water for long journeys or hikes to keep you energized and hydrated throughout the day.

Travel Pillow and Eye Mask:

If you have a long flight or are taking road trips, a travel pillow and eye mask will help you get some rest and arrive at your destination feeling refreshed.

Finally, don't forget to bring a reusable water bottle to stay hydrated while on the go. Tap water is safe to drink in

Bulgaria, and this eco-friendly choice will help you reduce plastic waste.

Sofia: The Capital City

Top Attractions in Sofia

Sofia, the vibrant capital of Bulgaria, is a treasure trove of history, culture, and natural beauty. With its ancient tales and modern developments, Sofia is a captivating destination for all travelers. From awe-inspiring religious sites to majestic mountain landscapes, the city has something for everyone. Let's explore the top attractions in Sofia, where history, art, and nature come together to create a memorable experience.

The Alexander Nevsky Cathedral is an iconic symbol of Sofia. This magnificent Orthodox cathedral was built in the early 20th century to honor the Russian soldiers who lost their lives during the Russo-Turkish War of 1877-1878, which led to Bulgaria's liberation from Ottoman rule. The cathedral's neo-Byzantine style features intricate golden domes, white marble, and detailed mosaics, making it a true work of art. Inside, visitors can admire religious icons, frescoes, and a mesmerizing central dome. The cathedral's crypt houses an impressive collection of religious artifacts, including precious icons and relics. Whether you're a history enthusiast, an architecture admirer, or a spiritual seeker, the Alexander Nevsky Cathedral is a must-visit destination in Sofia.

Vitosha Mountain and National Park is a nature lover's paradise. Just a stone's throw away from Sofia's bustling city center, Vitosha is one of Bulgaria's most accessible and visited mountains. It is also a protected national park with diverse flora and fauna. During the warmer months, the mountain's hiking trails invite visitors to explore the lush forests and meadows adorned with wildflowers. The peak of Cherni Vrah provides a breathtaking panoramic view of Sofia and its surroundings. In winter, Vitosha transforms into a snow-capped wonderland, attracting skiers and snowboarders to its slopes. With its proximity to the city, Vitosha is an ideal destination for locals and tourists alike.

The Boyana Church is a historical gem nestled at the foot of Vitosha Mountain. This exquisite medieval Orthodox church, known for its remarkable frescoes, dates back to the 10th century, with later additions and renovations in the 13th and 19th centuries. Inside, visitors can admire three layers of frescoes, each reflecting a different era of Bulgarian art. Due to its historical and artistic significance, the church has a limited number of visitors allowed per day, so booking tickets in advance is highly recommended.

The National Palace of Culture (NDK) is a cultural and architectural marvel. Built in the 1980s to mark the country's 13th centenary, the NDK is a massive congress and exhibition center with a distinctive communist-era design. Its impressive facade features colossal columns and imposing sculptures, creating an aura of grandiosity. The center houses numerous event halls, theaters, galleries, and exhibition spaces, making it a hub of cultural, artistic, and entertainment activities. Surrounding the NDK, visitors can enjoy the sprawling South Park, a popular green oasis in Sofia.

The Ivan Vazov National Theatre is the pride of Sofia's cultural scene. Named after Bulgaria's beloved poet and playwright, Ivan Vazov, this majestic theater is the country's oldest and most prestigious theater. Established in 1904, the theater is one of the most stunning neo-classical buildings in the city. It is a vibrant cultural epicenter that hosts events for all interests.

Visiting the Ivan Vazov National Theatre is a unique experience that allows you to explore Bulgaria's artistic heritage. The theatre's facade is adorned with statues of famous Bulgarian writers and artists, setting the stage for the cultural treasures that lie within. Inside, you'll find opulent decorations, majestic chandeliers, and a lavish royal box. The main stage has seen countless iconic performances, from classic plays to contemporary productions, making it a focal point of Bulgaria's artistic legacy.

Attending a show at the theatre is an immersive experience that will give you a glimpse into Bulgaria's artistic soul. If you can't make it to a performance, you can still visit the theatre during the day to admire its architectural beauty.

Cultural Experiences in Sofia

As the vibrant capital of Bulgaria, Sofia is a city that is steeped in history, culture, and diverse traditions. From ancient landmarks to contemporary art scenes, the city offers a wealth of cultural experiences that captivate the hearts of travelers. During my exploration of Sofia, I was enchanted by its rich heritage and the seamless fusion of old and new, creating a unique tapestry of Bulgarian identity. Here are some of the most captivating cultural experiences that await you in Sofia:

Alexander Nevsky Cathedral:

A symbol of Sofia and an architectural marvel, the Alexander Nevsky Cathedral is a must-visit cultural site. This massive Orthodox cathedral stands with its golden domes and ornate façade, drawing visitors from all over the world. Inside, the cathedral's interior is adorned with stunning frescoes and intricate iconography, creating an atmosphere of spiritual reverence. As I stood in awe of the cathedral's grandeur, I witnessed locals lighting candles and offering prayers, reflecting the deep-rooted religious practices that have shaped Bulgaria's culture.

National History Museum:

To delve deeper into Bulgaria's past, I visited the National History Museum, a treasure trove of artifacts and exhibits that span the country's extensive history. Housed in the former residence of the Communist Party's Central Committee, the museum showcases archaeological finds, medieval treasures, and artifacts from ancient civilizations that have thrived in the region. As I walked through its halls, I gained insights into Bulgaria's cultural evolution, from its Thracian roots to its Ottoman and Soviet periods.

Ivan Vazov National Theatre:

For a taste of Sofia's thriving arts scene, attending a performance at the Ivan Vazov National Theatre is a must. As the oldest and most prestigious theater in Bulgaria, it showcases an impressive repertoire of plays, operas, and ballets. The theater's neoclassical façade and elegant interiors add to the cultural ambiance, making it a cultural gem that celebrates the performing arts, a significant aspect of Bulgarian culture.

Museum of Socialist Art:

Sofia's history as a former communist state is intriguing, and the Museum of Socialist Art offers a glimpse into that era. The museum houses a collection of socialist-era sculptures and artifacts, including pieces removed from public spaces after the fall of communism. This unique museum provides an opportunity to reflect on Bulgaria's political past and its influence on the nation's cultural identity.

National Palace of Culture:

The National Palace of Culture, or NDK, is a modern architectural masterpiece that serves as a hub for cultural events and exhibitions. It hosts numerous international festivals, concerts, and conferences, making it a center for cultural exchange. I had the pleasure of attending a cultural festival here, where I witnessed traditional Bulgarian music and dance performances, further immersing myself in the country's rich cultural heritage.

Boyana Church:

A UNESCO World Heritage Site, Boyana Church is an exquisite example of Bulgarian medieval art and architecture. Its interior boasts impressive frescoes dating back to the 10th century, portraying biblical scenes and historical events. The church's preservation of this ancient art form is a testament to Bulgaria's dedication to its cultural heritage.

Sofia History Museum:

Located in the heart of Sofia, the Sofia History Museum offers a comprehensive look at the city's development over the centuries. Exhibits display artifacts, photographs, and documents that trace Sofia's history from Roman times to the present day. It was fascinating to witness how the city has evolved, combining ancient landmarks with modern urban development, showcasing Sofia's cultural resilience.

Bulgarian Cuisine and Wine Tasting:

No cultural experience in Sofia is complete without indulging in traditional Bulgarian cuisine. The city's culinary scene reflects its diverse cultural influences, blending Eastern and Western flavors. I had the pleasure of savoring dishes like banitsa (a flaky pastry filled with cheese), kavarma (a slow-cooked meat stew), and rakia (a traditional fruit brandy). Pairing these delicacies with Bulgarian wines was a delight, as the country boasts several wine regions known for producing exceptional vintages.

St. Nedelya Square and Sofia Synagogue:

St. Nedelya Square is a bustling public space in the heart of Sofia, surrounded by architectural wonders like the St. Nedelya Church and the Sofia Synagogue. The synagogue is one of the largest in Europe and showcases Sofia's rich Jewish heritage. Visiting these sites allowed me to witness the harmonious coexistence of different cultural and religious communities in the city.

Vitosha Boulevard in Sofia is a vibrant street where the old and the new come together. It's full of stores, cafes, and eateries, making it a great place to hang out and people watch. I had a great time strolling around, checking out the local shops, and getting a taste of the city's modern culture.

Plovdiv: The City of Seven Hills

Must-Visit Places in Plovdiv

Nestled in the heart of Bulgaria, Plovdiv is a city that has been around for thousands of years and is full of culture, architecture, and art. It was even named the European Capital of Culture in 2019! One of the most captivating places in Plovdiv is the Old Town, where you can take a step back in time and explore the city's ancient history.

One of the must-see spots in the Old Town is the Plovdiv Ancient Theatre, a stunning amphitheater that was built during the reign of Emperor Trajan in the 2nd century AD. It could hold up to 7,000 people and was used for theatrical plays, gladiator fights, and musical events. Nowadays, it has been restored and continues to host cultural events, concerts, and the International Festival of Opera and Ballet.

Another incredible sight in Plovdiv's Old Town is Nebet Tepe, an ancient hill that has been inhabited since the 6th millennium BC. It has served as a fortress for many civilizations, including the Thracians, Romans, Byzantines, and Ottomans. Climbing to the top of Nebet Tepe will give you a breathtaking view of the city and its surroundings.

The Roman Stadium is another must-visit historical site in Plovdiv. It was built in the 2nd century AD and could accommodate up to 30,000 spectators. It was mainly used for gladiator contests and athletic competitions. Now, visitors can explore the well-preserved remains of the stadium and learn about the grandeur of the Roman Empire.

Plovdiv is also a modern cultural hub, and the Kapana Creative District is a great example of this. This area was historically a center for craftsmen and artisans, but it has been transformed into a vibrant neighborhood with art galleries, boutiques, cafes, and workshops. During the Kapana Fest, you can experience the city's contemporary cultural scene and enjoy art exhibitions, live performances, and interactive events. Plus, Kapana is a great place to sample traditional Bulgarian dishes and international cuisine.

Art and Festivals in Plovdiv

Plovdiv long history, dating back thousands of years, is reflected in its vibrant art scene and celebrated through a variety of festivals and events that attract both locals and visitors. As the European Capital of Culture in 2019, Plovdiv has only increased its commitment to promoting art and culture, making it a must-visit destination for art lovers and festival-goers from all over the world.

The artistic spirit of Plovdiv is evident everywhere, from its stunning architecture to its lively street art. As you wander through the cobbled streets of the Old Town, you'll come across galleries, studios, and creative spaces that showcase the works of local and international artists. The city's art scene is incredibly diverse, with influences from traditional Bulgarian art to contemporary and experimental forms.

Plovdiv is home to many art galleries that feature rotating exhibitions of paintings, sculptures, and multimedia installations. The City Art Gallery, located in the iconic Nedkovich House, displays a vast collection of Bulgarian art from the 19th and 20th centuries, as well as temporary exhibitions that bring fresh perspectives and contemporary art forms to the forefront.

For a more immersive experience, visit the Kapana Creative District, a vibrant neighborhood full of art studios, design shops, and galleries. Kapana, meaning "the trap," got its name from the labyrinthine streets that once trapped visitors. Today, it has become a haven for artists, designers, and creative minds who have transformed the district into an open-air art gallery.

Plovdiv's streets serve as an ever-changing canvas for local and international street artists. You'll find colorful murals and graffiti adorning buildings, walls, and underpasses, adding an artistic flair to the city's urban landscape. Many of these murals reflect social and political themes, while others celebrate the city's cultural heritage. A street art tour is an excellent way to explore Plovdiv's creative side and discover hidden gems tucked away in unexpected corners.

One of Plovdiv's most remarkable art treasures is the Ancient Theater of Philippopolis, an ancient Roman amphitheater that has stood for over two millennia. Today, the theater serves as a cultural venue, hosting concerts, theatrical performances, and dance shows. Watching a performance in this historic setting under the starlit sky is a truly unforgettable experience.

Plovdiv's calendar is full of festivals that celebrate art, culture, music, and more. These events not only showcase the city's creative talents but also foster cultural exchange and bring communities together. The Plovdiv International Fair, held annually in early autumn, is one of the oldest and most significant trade fairs in Southeastern Europe. Originally established in 1892, the fair has evolved over the years to include cultural events, exhibitions, and entertainment. Plovdiv also participates in the European Night of Museums and Galleries, an event held on the

Saturday closest to International Museum Day in May. On this night, museums, galleries, and cultural institutions open their doors to the public until late at night, offering free admission and a range of special events and activities.

The Sound and Light Festival at the Ancient Theater of Philippopolis is another spectacular audiovisual event that takes place during the summer months. Using cutting-edge technology, the festival illuminates the ancient ruins with vibrant colors and projects captivating visuals onto the theater's ancient walls. This multisensory experience narrates the history of Plovdiv, transporting the audience back in time through an enchanting fusion of sound and light. Night/Plovdiv is an annual event that turns the city into an open-air stage for contemporary arts and performances. Artists, musicians, dancers, and performers take over the streets, squares, and parks, offering a diverse and immersive cultural experience. The festival celebrates art in all its forms and encourages interactions between artists and the public.

Kapana Fest is an amazing three-day event that celebrates art, design, and music in the Kapana Creative District. Local artists and designers showcase their work, while workshops, exhibitions, and live performances fill the streets. It's a vibrant display of Plovdiv's artistic spirit and its commitment to fostering creative expression.

Opera Open is an annual opera festival that takes place at the Ancient Theater of Philippopolis during the summer. It's a popular event that draws opera lovers from Bulgaria and beyond. Attendees are treated to classical opera performances in a stunning setting, making it a truly magical experience.

Varna: The Coastal Gem

Top Beaches in Varna

Varna, a stunning coastal city located on Bulgaria's Black Sea coast, is renowned for its beautiful beaches and vibrant seaside atmosphere. With its golden sands, clear waters, and a variety of beachside attractions, Varna is an idyllic destination for beach lovers and sun seekers. Let's explore the top beaches in Varna, including Golden Sands Beach and Sunny Day Beach, and discover the allure of these stunning coastal retreats.

Golden Sands Beach:

Golden Sands Beach, also known as Zlatni Pyasatsi, is one of the most popular and iconic beaches in Varna. Located just 17 kilometers north of Varna's city center, this magnificent beach stretches for over 3.5 kilometers along the Black Sea coast, providing plenty of space for visitors to soak up the sun and enjoy the sparkling waters.

a. **The Golden Sands**: As its name suggests, the beach boasts fine, golden sands that are soft to the touch, making it a delight for beachgoers to lounge and build sandcastles. The beach's expansive size ensures that even during peak seasons, it never feels overcrowded, allowing visitors to find their perfect spot to relax and unwind.

b. **Crystal Clear Waters:** The waters off Golden Sands Beach are clear and inviting, making it a fantastic spot for swimming and various water sports. The calm and shallow waters close to the shore are particularly appealing to families with children, providing a safe and enjoyable environment for all.

c. **Water Sports and Activities:** Golden Sands Beach offers a wide range of water sports and activities, catering to thrill-seekers and adventure enthusiasts. From jet skiing and parasailing to windsurfing and paddleboarding, there's something for everyone to enjoy.

d. **Beachfront Promenade:** Strolling along the beachfront promenade is a delightful experience. Lined with cafes, restaurants, and shops, it offers a pleasant atmosphere for leisurely walks, sunset views, and al fresco dining.

e. **Vibrant Nightlife**: As the sun sets, Golden Sands Beach transforms into a hub of nightlife and entertainment. Beach bars and clubs come alive with music, beach parties, and dancing, providing a lively and unforgettable experience for those looking to enjoy Varna's vibrant nightlife scene.

Sunny Day Beach:

Situated approximately 15 kilometers south of Varna's city center, Sunny Day Beach, or Slanchev Den Beach, offers a more tranquil and secluded beach experience compared to the bustling Golden Sands Beach. This charming stretch of coastline is an excellent choice for travelers seeking a quieter and more intimate escape.

a. **Secluded Paradise:** Sunny Day Beach is nestled in a secluded bay surrounded by lush greenery and rocky cliffs, creating a sense of serenity and seclusion. This makes it a perfect spot for those who wish to escape the crowds and immerse themselves in nature's beauty.

b. **Relaxation and Wellness:** Sunny Day Beach is adjacent to the Sunny Day Resort, a wellness-oriented complex that focuses on relaxation and rejuvenation. Visitors can indulge in spa treatments, yoga sessions, and wellness programs, making it an ideal destination for travelers seeking a holistic beach experience.

c. **Rocky Coves and Calm Waters:** The beach is characterized by its rocky coves and crystal-clear waters, providing a picturesque backdrop for tranquil moments and snorkeling adventures. Exploring the underwater world of Sunny Day Beach is a must for nature enthusiasts and sea lovers.

d. **Beachfront Dining**: The beach offers a few beachfront restaurants and bars, where visitors can savor delicious seafood dishes and refreshing beverages while admiring the panoramic views of the Black Sea.

e. **Nature Walks**: Surrounding the beach, there are scenic walking trails that lead to nearby cliffs and viewpoints, offering captivating vistas of the coastline and the vast sea beyond. Nature lovers will find ample opportunities to connect with the region's natural beauty.

Both Golden Sands Beach and Sunny Day Beach offer their unique allure, catering to different preferences and interests. Whether you seek vibrant beach parties and a lively atmosphere or peaceful seclusion and nature-oriented experiences, Varna's top beaches have something special to offer every visitor.

Tips for Enjoying the Beaches in Varna:

1. **Sun Protection**: Don't forget to pack sunscreen with a high SPF, a wide-brimmed hat, and sunglasses to protect yourself from the strong rays of the sun.

2. **Stay Hydrated**: Bring a reusable water bottle with you to make sure you stay hydrated throughout the day. It's especially important to drink lots of water during the hot summer months.

3. **Beach Gear**: Don't forget to bring all the beach essentials like a beach towel, swimwear, flip-flops, and a beach bag to make sure you have a comfortable beach day.

4. **Water Activities:** If you're interested in any water sports or activities, check with local providers for rental options and safety guidelines.

5. **Beachfront Dining:** Enjoy the beachside atmosphere by trying some of the local seafood dishes at the beachfront restaurants.

6. **Beach Cleanup:** Help keep these beaches beautiful by disposing of your trash properly and participating in beach cleanup efforts.

Bulgaria for Nature Lovers

Danube River and Wildlife Sanctuaries

The Danube River is a lifeline that runs through the very heart of Bulgaria, stretching for around 470 kilometers within the country's borders. It begins in the Black Forest of Germany and winds its way through ten countries before emptying into the Black Sea in Romania. As it enters Bulgaria, the river becomes a vital natural resource, influencing the landscape and providing essential habitats for a wide range of wildlife.

Throughout history, the Danube has been a major trade route, connecting civilizations and cultures for centuries. Today, it continues to be an important transportation artery, facilitating trade and tourism between countries. It has also inspired many artists, writers, and nature lovers, with its serenity and the remarkable diversity of life along its banks.

THE DANUBE IN BULGARIA: A NATURE LOVER'S PARADISE

As the Danube flows through Bulgaria, it forms picturesque bends, creating tranquil river landscapes that are home to numerous species of birds, fish, and mammals. One of the most remarkable stretches of the Danube in Bulgaria is the Danube Delta, which lies near the town of Silistra in the northern part of the country. This UNESCO Biosphere Reserve is a haven for biodiversity, housing more than 300 species of birds and an abundance of plant and animal life.

BULGARIAN WILDLIFE SANCTUARIES ALONG THE DANUBE

a. Srebarna Nature Reserve:

Located near the town of Srebarna, this exceptional wetland sanctuary is a UNESCO World Heritage Site and a Ramsar Wetland of International Importance. The reserve encompasses Lake Srebarna, a shallow freshwater lake that hosts one of Europe's most diverse bird populations. Here, birdwatchers can spot over 180 bird species, including the globally endangered Dalmatian pelican, white-tailed eagle, pygmy cormorant, and glossy ibis.

b. Persina Nature Park:

As the Danube flows further east, it encounters Persina Nature Park, another sanctuary of immense ecological importance. The park covers over 19,000 hectares, comprising riverine forests, meadows, and wetlands. Visitors can explore the park's diverse landscapes by boat, observing numerous bird species, such as the common tern, little egret, and ferruginous duck. The park is also home to various mammals, including deer, wild boars, and the elusive European otter.

c. Rusenski Lom Nature Park:

In the northeastern region of Bulgaria lies Rusenski Lom Nature Park, where the Danube has carved stunning limestone cliffs and canyons. This unique geological formation provides shelter for rare plant species, creating a lush ecosystem with an abundance of wildlife. Rare birds like the black stork, long-legged buzzard, and black vulture can be seen in the skies above the park. The picturesque medieval rock-hewn churches and fortresses within the park add to its historical and cultural significance.

EXPLORING THE DANUBE RIVER AND WILDLIFE SANCTUARIES

The Danube River and its associated wildlife sanctuaries offer a wealth of activities for nature lovers and adventurers alike:

Birdwatching: The Danube and its wetlands attract an impressive variety of birds, making it a birdwatcher's paradise. Visitors can take birdwatching excursions to spot rare and migratory bird species.

Boating and Cruises: River cruises along the Danube provide a serene and picturesque experience, allowing travelers to take in the natural beauty and observe wildlife along the riverbanks.

Hiking and Nature Walks: Many areas surrounding the Danube and its sanctuaries are crisscrossed with hiking trails and nature paths. These trails lead visitors through pristine landscapes and offer the chance to encounter the area's diverse flora and fauna up close.

Photography: From stunning sunrises and sunsets over the river to capturing the grace of birdlife in flight, the Danube and its wildlife sanctuaries offer excellent photography opportunities for both amateurs and professionals.

Exploring the Danube River and its surroundings can be a great way to uncover Bulgaria's cultural heritage. Historic towns, ancient ruins, and traditional villages are all located along the riverbanks, providing visitors with a unique insight into the country's past.

It is also important to remember that the preservation of the Danube River and its wildlife sanctuaries is of utmost importance. The Bulgarian government and environmental organizations are working hard to protect the fragile ecosystems and the diverse species that inhabit the region.

To ensure the natural beauty of the area is preserved, it is essential to follow marked trails, respect wildlife habitats, and adhere to waste management guidelines when visiting.

Strandzha Nature Park

The Strandzha Nature Park is a stunning wilderness that offers a unique and captivating experience for nature lovers and adventurers. Spanning an area of 1,161 square kilometers, Strandzha Nature Park is one of the largest protected areas in the country and is renowned for its abundant biodiversity, ancient forests, and mesmerizing landscapes.

A Haven of Biodiversity:

Strandzha Nature Park is a biodiversity hotspot, boasting a variety of ecosystems that support a wide range of flora and fauna. The park is characterized by lush forests, meandering rivers, and picturesque landscapes, making it a perfect habitat for many plant and animal species. Some of Bulgaria's rare and endangered species, such as the Strandzha fire salamander, thrive in this protected area.

The park is home to over 700 vascular plant species, including some that are exclusive to this region.

Throughout the seasons, visitors are treated to a riot of colors as the wildflowers bloom in the meadows and forests. The ancient Strandzha beech forests, some of which date back over 4,000 years, stand as a living testament to the park's ecological importance and historical value.

Wildlife Encounters:

Strandzha Nature Park is a sanctuary for an impressive diversity of wildlife, making it a paradise for birdwatchers and wildlife enthusiasts. Birdwatching in the park is a treat, as over 270 bird species have been recorded here, including the majestic golden eagle and the enchanting European roller. In the early mornings and evenings, the melodious songs of the nightingales fill the air, adding to the park's magical atmosphere.

Among the park's inhabitants are also mammals such as deer, wild boar, and the elusive Balkan lynx. Keep an eye out for tracks and signs of these elusive creatures as you explore the park's trails. If you're lucky, you might catch a glimpse of one of these majestic animals in their natural habitat.

Cultural and Historical Heritage:

The Strandzha Mountains have been inhabited by humans for thousands of years, and traces of their presence can be found throughout the park. The region is rich in cultural and historical heritage, with numerous ancient sanctuaries, Thracian burial mounds, and remnants of medieval fortifications scattered across the landscape.

One of the most intriguing cultural features is the Strandzha wooden houses, known as "mandra." These traditional houses with steep roofs, wooden verandas, and unique architectural style are still in use by the local people, preserving the authentic charm of the region.

Hiking and Outdoor Activities:

Strandzha Nature Park is a paradise for hikers and outdoor enthusiasts, offering a network of well-marked trails that lead through the park's diverse landscapes. The hiking trails vary in difficulty, catering to both casual walkers and experienced trekkers. Whether you choose a leisurely stroll through the ancient forests or a more challenging ascent to the park's highest peaks, every step is rewarded with breathtaking views and an immersive natural experience.

One of the popular hiking routes leads to the highest peak in the park, Mount Mahya. From its summit, hikers are treated to sweeping panoramic views of the lush greenery, the Black Sea coast, and even glimpses of neighboring Turkey.

Charming Villages and Local Culture:

Exploring the quaint villages nestled in the Strandzha Mountains is an excellent way to experience the local culture and hospitality of the region. The villages offer a glimpse into traditional Bulgarian rural life, with their cobblestone streets, well-preserved houses, and picturesque churches. The locals, known for their warm welcome, are proud of their heritage and are eager to share stories of their history and customs.

During your visit, you may have the opportunity to witness traditional folk festivals and cultural events, where you can enjoy the vibrant music, dance, and cuisine that are integral to the local way of life.

Environmental Conservation and Sustainable Tourism:

Strandzha Nature Park is a protected area, managed with the primary goal of environmental conservation and sustainable tourism. The park authorities work hard to preserve the delicate ecosystems, protect endangered species, and maintain the cultural heritage of the region.

If you're planning a trip to Strandzha Nature Park, here are some tips to help you make the most of your visit! Entry to the park is free, but you may need to get a permit from the park authorities if you plan to camp or join a guided tour. Guided tours are a great way to learn more about the park's flora, fauna, and history.

The best time to visit depends on what you're interested in - spring and early summer are great for wildflowers and birdwatching, while autumn brings a stunning display of fall colors. Be sure to bring water, snacks, a map, and a first aid kit, and be prepared for changing weather conditions.

There are no hotels or resorts within the park, but you can find charming guesthouses and traditional accommodations in the surrounding villages. Enjoy your visit and remember to practice responsible tourism - stay on marked trails, don't litter, and respect the natural and cultural heritage of the area.

Vitosha Mountain: Hiking and Outdoor Adventures

Bulgaria's capital city, Sofia, Vitosha Mountain stands tall as a majestic playground for nature lovers and outdoor adventurers. This haven of natural beauty and diverse landscapes offers a plethora of activities throughout the year, making it an ideal destination for hiking, skiing, and immersing oneself in the pristine wilderness. Vitosha is one of the oldest national parks in the Balkans and is a favorite among locals seeking respite from urban life, as well as a must-visit destination for travelers looking to experience Bulgaria's untouched beauty.

At an elevation of 2,290 meters (7,513 feet) at its highest peak, Cherni Vrah (Black Peak), Vitosha Mountain is easily accessible for day trips or longer excursions, allowing visitors to experience the best of both urban and natural wonders. The mountain's unique blend of alpine meadows, rugged terrain, and ancient forests creates an enchanting landscape that beckons adventurers and nature lovers year-round.

Vitosha Mountain boasts an extensive network of well-marked hiking trails suitable for all levels of hikers, from beginners to experienced trekkers. For those seeking a leisurely stroll through nature, the lower parts of the mountain offer gentle trails, such as the Golden Bridges Eco-Trail, which meanders through lush forests and picturesque meadows, leading to the symbolic "Golden Bridges" rock formations. More experienced hikers can tackle the ascent to Cherni Vrah, the highest point of Vitosha. The trail offers a challenging yet rewarding climb, surrounded by breathtaking panoramas at every turn. The journey to the top takes you through alpine landscapes and allows you to witness the incredible biodiversity of the mountain, with over 1,000 plant species and various wildlife, including deer, boars, and eagles.

During the winter months, Vitosha Mountain transforms into a winter wonderland, attracting skiers and snowboarders to its snow-covered slopes. The mountain features several ski runs catering to different skill levels, and ski resorts like Aleko and Konyarnika offer amenities such as ski equipment rentals and cozy chalets. The snow-capped peaks provide an unforgettable backdrop for a day of skiing or snowboarding, and the proximity to Sofia makes it a popular destination for winter sports enthusiasts.

One of the most rewarding aspects of visiting Vitosha Mountain is the panoramic views it offers. Whether you're hiking the trails, enjoying a scenic chairlift ride, or standing atop Cherni Vrah, the vistas are nothing short of awe-inspiring. On clear days, you can see the city of Sofia spread out below, while the surrounding mountains and valleys create a captivating tapestry of nature's beauty.

Vitosha Mountain has been a protected area since 1934, and its conservation is of utmost importance to Bulgaria's natural heritage. As a designated national park, the mountain is home to unique flora and fauna, some of which are endemic to the region. Visitors are encouraged to follow the principles of "Leave No Trace" and respect the environment by not leaving any litter and staying on designated paths.

Beyond hiking and skiing, Vitosha Mountain offers a myriad of other outdoor activities for the adventurous. Mountain biking enthusiasts will find thrilling trails that wind through the forests and meadows, offering an adrenaline-pumping experience surrounded by nature's beauty. Rock climbing enthusiasts can test their skills on the various cliffs and rock faces scattered across the mountain. Local climbing schools and guides are available for those seeking to explore this exciting aspect of Vitosha. Nature lovers can embark on wildlife-watching expeditions, seeking out the diverse fauna that calls the mountain home. Birdwatching is particularly rewarding, with various bird species, including the elusive wallcreeper and majestic golden eagle, spotted within the park's boundaries.

For travelers seeking relaxation and rejuvenation, Vitosha Mountain offers ample opportunities for wellness and recreation. The clean mountain air and serene surroundings make it an ideal place for yoga retreats, meditation sessions, and forest bathing experiences. Many wellness centers and eco-lodges provide a perfect escape from the hustle and bustle of everyday life.

Exploring Vitosha Mountain is easy and convenient from Sofia. The Simeonovo Gondola Lift and Dragalevtsi Chairlift provide a scenic ride to the higher parts of the mountain, while buses and taxis can take you to the base. However, it's important to prioritize safety when you're out there.

Make sure to check the weather forecast before you go, and let someone know your plans and estimated return time. Don't forget to bring enough water, snacks, a map, and a fully charged phone in case of an emergency.

Bulgarian Cuisine and Food Experiences

Traditional Bulgarian Dishes

Traditional recipes have been passed down through generations, making Bulgarian dishes a treat for both the taste buds and the soul. Here are seven traditional Bulgarian dishes that epitomize the country's culinary heritage.

Shopska Salad:

This is one of the most popular Bulgarian dishes, and it's a refreshing delight, especially during the hot summer months. It's made with simple yet flavorful ingredients, such as fresh tomatoes, cucumbers, onions, and roasted peppers, all finely chopped. The dish is then topped with grated sirene, a white brined cheese with a slightly salty taste. A drizzle of olive oil and a sprinkling of dried herbs, usually parsley or dill, complete this colorful and healthy salad. Shopska Salad is a true representation of Bulgarian hospitality and is served as a starter or accompaniment to main meals.

Banitsa:

Banitsa is a beloved Bulgarian pastry that holds a special place in the hearts of locals. This delicious dish consists of layers of filo pastry brushed with butter and filled with a mixture of whisked eggs and Bulgarian feta cheese (sirene). Sometimes, yogurt or spinach is added to the filling, creating delightful variations. The layers are then rolled and baked until golden and crispy. Banitsa is often enjoyed for breakfast or as a traditional dish during family gatherings and holidays. It is a symbol of good luck and prosperity, making it a must-have during significant celebrations.

Kavarma:

Kavarma is a hearty and aromatic stew, typically made with pork or chicken, and often with a combination of various vegetables. The meat is slowly cooked in a clay pot with onions, tomatoes, bell peppers, mushrooms, and garlic, allowing the flavors to meld into a comforting and flavorful dish. Kavarma is seasoned with a mix of Bulgarian spices and herbs, such as thyme and paprika, giving it a uniquely Bulgarian taste. It is often served with a side of rice or crusty bread to soak up the delicious sauce.

Tarator:

Tarator is a refreshing and light cold soup, perfect for cooling down during Bulgaria's hot summers. This traditional dish consists of yogurt, cucumbers, garlic, dill, and sometimes walnuts, all blended into a creamy and tangy soup. It is garnished with fresh cucumbers and a drizzle of olive oil. Tarator is not only delicious but also incredibly healthy, providing a cooling respite on warm days.

Sarmi:

Sarmi, also known as stuffed cabbage rolls, is a cherished Bulgarian dish that has been a part of the country's culinary heritage for centuries. To make sarmi, tender cabbage leaves are filled with a savory mixture of minced meat (often a combination of pork and beef), rice, onions, and spices. The stuffed cabbage rolls are then simmered in a tomato-based sauce until tender and flavorful. Sarmi is a classic dish served during holidays, family gatherings, and special occasions, reflecting the importance of tradition and community in Bulgarian culture.

Meshana Skara:

Meshana Skara, which translates to "mixed grill," is a meat lover's dream come true. This hearty dish consists of an assortment of grilled meats, such as pork, chicken, kebapche (spiced minced meat), and kyufte (meatballs). The meats are seasoned with a blend of Bulgarian spices and served with a side of Shopska Salad and freshly baked bread. Meshana Skara is a popular choice for a hearty and satisfying meal, perfect for sharing with friends and family.

Kozunak:

Kozunak is a traditional Bulgarian sweet bread, typically baked during Easter and other special occasions. This rich and fragrant bread is made with eggs, butter, sugar, and milk, and is studded with raisins and sometimes walnuts. Kozunak is beautifully braided and decorated before being baked to perfection. It is often enjoyed as a dessert or as a symbol of abundance and prosperity during festive gatherings.

Culinary Tours and Cooking Classes

Exploring Bulgarian cuisine is a delightful and immersive experience, and culinary tourism has become increasingly popular in the country. From hearty stews to savory pastries and sweet delights, here are five traditional Bulgarian dishes you can learn to prepare during culinary tours and cooking classes.

1. **Kavarma** is a comforting and aromatic stew made with pork or chicken, marinated and cooked in a clay pot with vegetables and Bulgarian spices.
2. **Banitsa** is a beloved pastry made with layers of filo dough, butter, and a mixture of whisked eggs and Bulgarian feta cheese.
3. **Tarator** is a refreshing cold soup made with yogurt, cucumbers, garlic, dill, and sometimes walnuts.
4. **Sarmi** is a traditional dish of stuffed cabbage rolls filled with minced meat, rice, onions, and spices.
5. **Skara** is a carnivore's delight of grilled meats seasoned with Bulgarian spices and herbs.

Bulgaria for Families and Kids

Family-Friendly Attractions and Activities

Bulgaria is a Balkan gem that offers something for everyone, no matter their age. From exploring historic cities to enjoying outdoor adventures, there's a plethora of family-friendly attractions and activities to choose from.

Sunny Beach is the perfect destination for a fun-filled family vacation, with its long stretch of golden sandy beach and thrilling water sports. Rila Monastery is a captivating cultural experience, with its intricate frescoes and ancient icons.

Plovdiv's Old Town is like stepping back in time, with its cobbled streets and colorful houses. Vitosha Mountain is a wonderful escape into nature, with its lush forests and scenic meadows.

Pamporovo Ski Resort is perfect for kids and beginners learning to ski, and the Varna Dolphinarium is a delightful experience for children and animal lovers. Adventure parks offer thrilling activities for families seeking outdoor excitement, and children's museums provide interactive exhibits and workshops.

At **Zlatni Pyasatsi Nature Park**, located near the Golden Sands resort, families can take a peaceful stroll through the park's lush greenery and picturesque scenery. The park also houses the Aladzha Monastery, an old cave monastery that adds a hint of mystery to the visit. Kids will have a blast exploring the natural caves and discovering the history of this special place.

For a truly enriching experience, families can take part in traditional Bulgarian crafts and workshops. Many towns and villages across the country offer workshops where kids can learn to make pottery, paint traditional Easter eggs, or try their hand at wood carving. These hands-on activities give a unique insight into Bulgarian culture and customs.

Bulgarian Fairytales and Storytelling

The art of storytelling is deeply embedded in Bulgarian culture, with tales being passed down through generations. This cherished tradition has been around for centuries, with Griots, or storytellers, being highly respected in villages. These gifted individuals would gather around the village fire or in local gatherings, spinning captivating tales that transported listeners to magical realms and imparted valuable life lessons.

Bulgarian fairytales are a diverse collection of stories, each with its own unique themes and characters. These tales often draw inspiration from nature, animals, and mythical creatures, reflecting the country's varied landscapes and beliefs. Heroes and heroines, magical creatures, and folklore and legends are all common elements in these stories, which have adapted to changing times and remain beloved by Bulgarians.

Some of the most iconic Bulgarian fairytales include "The Enchanted Ring", "The Magic Pomegranate", and "The

Brave Slave". To celebrate this rich storytelling heritage, Bulgaria hosts various festivals and cultural events, such as the International Festival of Myth and Contemporary Art in Yambol. In addition, storytelling is still cherished in schools, cultural centers, and local gatherings, ensuring that these treasured narratives remain alive in the hearts and minds of Bulgarians.

Modern adaptations and preservation efforts are also being made to keep these age-old tales alive. Artists, writers, and filmmakers are reimagining these stories for contemporary audiences while staying true to their essence. Through these efforts, Bulgarian fairytales will continue to enchant both young and old, leaving a lasting imprint on the country's rich cultural heritage.

Traveling on a Budget

Affordable Accommodation Options

Bulgaria is a great destination for travelers looking for comfortable and affordable accommodation. Whether you're visiting the vibrant cities, relaxing on the Black Sea coast, or exploring the picturesque countryside, there are plenty of budget-friendly hotels that won't break the bank. Here are eight of the best affordable hotels in Bulgaria, along with their locations, pros, and cons:

Sofia Plaza Hotel (Sofia)

Right in the heart of Sofia, just a short walk from the city's main attractions, including Alexander Nevsky Cathedral and Vitosha Boulevard.

Pros: The hotel is in a great location, making it easy to explore Sofia on foot. The rooms are clean and comfortable, and the staff is friendly and helpful. Plus, there's an on-site restaurant serving delicious Bulgarian cuisine.

Cons: Some rooms may be on the smaller side, and noise from the nearby bustling streets can be heard at times.

Hotel City Avenue (Plovdiv)

Located in Plovdiv, close to the Old Town and many cultural landmarks, such as the Ancient Theatre of Philippopolis.

Pros: Hotel City Avenue is in a great spot for sightseeing, and the rooms are spacious and well-maintained. There's also a lovely garden terrace, perfect for relaxing after a day of exploring.

Cons: The breakfast buffet may have limited options compared to larger hotels.

Graffit Gallery Hotel (Varna)

Right in the heart of Varna, close to the Sea Garden Park and the Black Sea coast.

Pros: Graffit Gallery Hotel has modern and stylish rooms with artistic decor. The hotel's rooftop terrace offers stunning views of the city and the sea. Plus, there's an on-site spa and wellness center for a relaxing experience.

Cons: As a more upscale hotel, the prices may be slightly higher compared to other affordable options.

Hotel Bisser (Bansko)

Located in Bansko, a popular ski resort town in the Pirin Mountains.

Pros: Hotel Bisser is a great choice for budget-conscious travelers who want to enjoy winter sports. The hotel provides a cozy atmosphere, and the staff is accommodating. It's within walking distance to the ski lift and Bansko's charming town center.

Cons: The hotel's amenities may not be as luxurious as some higher-priced options.

Hotel Akroza (Ruse)

Situated in Ruse, close to the city center and the Danube River.

Pros: Hotel Akroza offers comfortable and clean rooms at an affordable price. The hotel's location provides easy access to Ruse's historical landmarks and lively streets. The staff is welcoming and eager to assist with travel inquiries.

Cons: The facilities may be more basic compared to larger hotels.

Saint Thomas Holiday Village (Sunny Beach)

Located in Sunny Beach, a popular resort destination on the Black Sea coast.

Pros: Saint Thomas Holiday Village is a great budget-friendly option for travelers seeking a seaside getaway. The hotel offers spacious apartments with kitchenettes, making it ideal for families or those who prefer self-catering options. The hotel has a swimming pool and is a short walk from the beach.

Cons: Sunny Beach can get crowded and noisy during the peak tourist season.

Hotel Trakietz (Veliko Tarnovo)

Situated in Veliko Tarnovo, a picturesque city known for its historic charm.

Pros: Hotel Trakietz provides a cozy and charming stay in Veliko Tarnovo. The hotel is close to the Old Town and Tsarevets Fortress, making it convenient for exploring the city's attractions. The rooms are comfortable, and the staff is welcoming.

Cons: The hotel may have fewer amenities compared to larger hotels.

Family Hotel Veronika (Bansko)

Located in Bansko, near the ski lift and Bansko's town center.

Pros: Family Hotel Veronika offers a warm and friendly atmosphere, making guests feel at home. The hotel is within walking distance to restaurants, shops, and ski facilities. The staff is attentive and provides personalized service.

Cons: The hotel's facilities may not be as extensive as some larger resorts.

Budget-Friendly Eateries

The country is renowned for its diverse and flavorful cuisine, and there are plenty of eateries that offer delicious meals without breaking the bank. From traditional Bulgarian dishes to international flavors, these budget-friendly restaurants cater to all tastes and guarantee a satisfying dining experience. Here are five top-notch eateries in Bulgaria that offer excellent value for money:

Happy Bar & Grill:

Multiple locations across Bulgaria, with branches in Sofia, Plovdiv, Varna, Burgas, and more.

Pros:

- **Wide Variety of Dishes:** Happy Bar & Grill has an extensive menu featuring a range of dishes, including Bulgarian classics, grilled meats, pizzas, and salads. There's something for everyone here!
- **Affordable Prices**: The prices at Happy Bar & Grill are wallet-friendly, making it a great choice for

travelers on a budget. Portions are generous, offering great value for money.

- **Family-Friendly:** This restaurant is perfect for families, as it provides a kids' menu and a pleasant atmosphere, making it a hit with both young and adult diners.

Cons:

- **Busy During Peak Hours:** Due to its popularity, Happy Bar & Grill can get crowded during peak dining hours. It's best to arrive early or make a reservation to secure a table.
- **Limited Authenticity**: While the restaurant offers a mix of Bulgarian and international dishes, some purists might prefer more authentic, locally-focused eateries.

Mehana Chuchura:

Mehana is located at 15 D-r Plovdiv St., Sofia

Pros:

- **Traditional Atmosphere:** Mehana Chuchura immerses diners in a traditional Bulgarian setting with rustic decor and live folk music, offering an authentic cultural experience.
- **Bulgarian Cuisine:** The menu at Mehana Chuchura focuses on traditional Bulgarian dishes, such as hearty stews, grilled meats, and appetizers like Shopska Salad and Banitsa.
- **Affordable Prices**: Despite its traditional ambiance, Mehana Chuchura offers reasonably priced meals, allowing visitors to savor Bulgarian cuisine without breaking the bank.

Cons:

- **Limited English Menu**: While staff members are generally helpful, the menu might have limited English translations, which could make ordering a bit challenging for non-Bulgarian speakers.

- **Potential Wait Times**: The restaurant's popularity can result in wait times during busy hours. It's advisable to make a reservation or arrive early for a more seamless dining experience.

Happy Sushi:

Happy Sushi is located at 45 Vitosha Blvd., Sofia

Pros:

- **Diverse Sushi Selection**: Happy Sushi offers an array of freshly made sushi rolls, nigiri, and sashimi. It's an excellent option for sushi lovers seeking a budget-friendly meal.
- **Quick Service**: The restaurant provides efficient service, ideal for travelers looking for a quick and delicious bite to eat before continuing their explorations.
- **Budget Sushi Sets:** Happy Sushi offers value-for-money sushi sets that include a variety of rolls and nigiri, making it a cost-effective way to sample different flavors.

Cons:

- **Limited Seating:** The restaurant might have limited seating space during busy hours, so it's advisable to plan your visit accordingly.
- **Not Exclusive to Bulgarian Cuisine:** While Happy Sushi offers delicious sushi, it may not cater to travelers specifically seeking traditional Bulgarian dishes.

Hadjidraganov's Houses:

Hadjidraganov is located at 75 Kozloduy St., Sofia

Pros:

- **Unique Ambiance:** Hadjidraganov's Houses is designed to resemble a traditional Bulgarian village, offering diners a unique and immersive cultural experience.
- **Authentic Bulgarian Dishes**: The menu showcases an array of authentic Bulgarian dishes, prepared with care and attention to detail, allowing visitors to indulge in genuine Bulgarian flavors.

- **Live Music and Entertainment:** The restaurant occasionally hosts live music and folk performances, adding to the overall dining experience and cultural immersion.

Cons:

- **Higher Price Range:** Hadjidraganov's Houses is relatively more upscale compared to other budget-friendly eateries. However, the experience and ambiance make it worth considering for a special meal.
- **Reservation Recommended:** Given its popularity and limited seating, making a reservation in advance is advisable, especially for dinner.

Patisserie Shtastlivetsa:

Patisserie is located at18 Patriarh Evtimiy Blvd., Sofia

Exploring Bulgaria's culinary scene can be a thrilling adventure, especially for those on a budget. The country is renowned for its rich and diverse cuisine, and there are plenty of eateries that offer delicious meals without breaking the bank. From traditional Bulgarian dishes to international flavors, these budget-friendly restaurants cater to all palates and guarantee a satisfying dining experience. Here are five top-notch eateries in Bulgaria that offer excellent value for money:

Happy Bar & Grill:

Multiple locations across Bulgaria, with branches in Sofia, Plovdiv, Varna, Burgas, and more.

Pros:

- **Wide Menu Selection:** Happy Bar & Grill has an extensive menu featuring a variety of dishes, including Bulgarian classics, grilled meats, pizzas, and salads. There's something for everyone here!
- **Affordable Prices:** The prices at Happy Bar & Grill are wallet-friendly, making it an excellent choice for travelers on a budget. Portions are generous, offering great value for money.
- **Family-Friendly:** This restaurant is well-suited for families, as it provides a kids' menu and a pleasant

ambiance, making it a hit with both young and adult diners.

Cons:

- **Busy During Peak Hours:** Due to its popularity, Happy Bar & Grill can get crowded during peak dining hours. It's best to arrive early or make a reservation to secure a table.
- **Limited Authenticity:** While the restaurant offers a mix of Bulgarian and international dishes, some purists might prefer more authentic, locally-focused eateries.

Free and Low-Cost Activities

Bulgaria is a Balkan gem that offers a wealth of opportunities for travelers to immerse themselves in its rich history, breathtaking landscapes, and vibrant culture. There are plenty of free and low-cost activities that allow you to experience the best of Bulgaria without overspending. Here are five budget-friendly activities that will make your Bulgarian adventure unforgettable.

Exploring Historic Cities: Bulgaria is home to a plethora of historic cities, each with its own unique stories and architectural wonders. In Sofia, the capital city, you can stroll through the city center to see iconic landmarks such as the Alexander Nevsky Cathedral, Saint Sofia Church, and the Rotunda of St. George. Plovdiv is a city of history and culture, with a beautifully preserved Old Town that dates back to Roman times.

Wander through its narrow cobbled streets, visit the Ancient Theatre, and admire the colorful houses of the Kapana Creative District. Veliko Tarnovo, known as the City of Tsars, offers a glimpse into Bulgaria's medieval past. The Tsarevets Fortress, with its stunning panoramic views, is a must-visit. Ruse, located on the banks of the Danube River, is known for its beautiful Belle Époque architecture. Take a leisurely walk along the riverside promenade and admire the elegant buildings. Koprivshtitsa is a charming town with well-preserved Bulgarian Revival architecture. Although some museums in the town require an entrance fee, you can still wander through its picturesque streets and admire the traditional houses.

Hiking in Nature's Wonderland: Bulgaria is a paradise for nature lovers, and the best part is that hiking is a budget-friendly activity that allows you to fully appreciate the country's stunning landscapes. The Rila Mountains feature a series of glacial lakes, each with its unique charm. The Pirin National Park is a UNESCO World Heritage Site and a haven for hikers.

The ascent to Vihren Peak, the second-highest summit in Bulgaria, rewards you with panoramic vistas of the rugged mountain terrain. Vitosha Mountain, located just outside the capital city of Sofia, offers various hiking trails. Strandzha Nature Park, located near the Black Sea coast, features lush forests, meandering rivers, and charming villages. The Rhodope Mountains, known for their mystical charm, offer a range of hiking routes suitable for all ages.

Exploring Bulgaria's Black Sea Coast:

If you're looking for a cost-effective way to relax and unwind, then Bulgaria's Black Sea coast is the perfect destination. Many of the beaches along the coast are free to access, so you can soak up the sun and take a dip in the sea without spending a dime. Here are some of the best beaches to explore:

a. **Golden Sands Beach**: This iconic beach near Varna is renowned for its golden sandy shores and crystal-clear waters. Take a leisurely stroll along the coast to discover hidden coves and rock formations.

b. **Sunny Beach:** As one of the largest and most popular resort areas on the Black Sea coast, Sunny Beach offers plenty of free beachfront space for sunbathing and swimming.

c. **Sozopol:** The charming town of Sozopol boasts beautiful beaches with a mix of sandy stretches and rocky coves. Take a stroll through the Old Town and explore its narrow streets, traditional houses, and quaint restaurants.

d. **Albena Beach:** Albena is a family-friendly resort known for its sandy beach and shallow waters, making it an ideal spot for children to play safely.

e. **Dyuni Beach**: Dyuni is a quieter and less crowded beach, perfect for those seeking a tranquil coastal experience.

Experience Bulgarian Culture:

Bulgaria's cultural calendar is filled with various festivals and events that showcase the country's traditions, music, and arts. Many of these events are either free to attend or have low admission fees, so you can experience Bulgarian culture up close. Here are some of the best cultural events and festivals to check out:

a. **Kukeri Festivals:** Kukeri festivals, held in various regions of Bulgaria, are colorful and lively events where participants wear elaborate masks and costumes to chase away evil spirits and welcome the arrival of spring.

b. **Rose Festival:** Celebrated in the Rose Valley region of Kazanlak, the Rose Festival is a joyous event that pays tribute to Bulgaria's rose-growing heritage. Visitors can watch the beautiful Rose Queen pageant and join the traditional rose-picking festivities.

c. **National Folklore Festivals:** Throughout the year, Bulgaria hosts numerous folklore festivals where dance troupes and musicians from different regions perform traditional Bulgarian music and dances.

d. **Varna International Ballet Competition**: Ballet enthusiasts can enjoy world-class performances by young dancers from around the globe during the Varna International Ballet Competition, held every two years in Varna.

e. Rhythms of the World Festival: The Rhythms of the World Festival in Plovdiv celebrates music, dance, and art from various cultures, bringing together performers from different countries for a lively and multicultural event.

Taste Bulgaria's Wines:

Bulgaria has a long history of winemaking, and wine tasting is an enjoyable and affordable activity that allows you to savor the country's excellent wines. Many wineries offer guided tours and wine tastings, so you can learn about the winemaking process and sample local varieties. Here are some of the best places to go wine tasting:

a. **Melnik:** Visit the town of Melnik, famous for its sand pyramids and impressive wine cellars. Explore the region's wineries and taste the renowned Melnik wine, made from the local broadleaf grape.

b. **Plovdiv Wine Tours**: Plovdiv and its surrounding areas are home to several wineries producing excellent wines.

Take a wine tour and savor Bulgarian red, white, and rosé wines.

c. **Thracian Valley:** The Thracian Valley is one of Bulgaria's prime wine regions, and its wineries welcome visitors for wine tastings. Enjoy the region's robust red wines and aromatic whites.

d. **Black Sea Coast Wineries**: Along the Black Sea coast, there are wineries producing unique wines with maritime influences. The region is known for its milder climate, which is favorable for growing specific grape varieties.

e. **Wine Festivals**: Keep an eye out for wine festivals held across the country, where you can taste a wide selection of wines and discover new favorites.

Conclusion

My journey to Bulgaria was an experience I will never forget. I had the chance to explore the country's rich history and culture, and I was fortunate enough to meet some amazing people along the way.

My trip began in Sofia, the capital city. I visited the Alexander Nevsky Cathedral, Vitosha Mountain, and the Boyana Church. I also had the pleasure of trying some delicious Bulgarian food at a local restaurant.

From Sofia, I went to Plovdiv, the second-largest city in Bulgaria. Plovdiv is a UNESCO World Heritage Site, and it is home to a number of ancient ruins. I visited the Roman Amphitheater, the Old Town, and the Plovdiv History Museum.

I also spent some time exploring the Bulgarian countryside. I visited the Rila Monastery, one of the most important monasteries in Bulgaria. I also went hiking in the Rila Mountains, and I visited the Seven Rila Lakes.

My trip ended in Varna, a popular seaside resort town. I spent my days swimming in the Black Sea, and I went on a boat trip to the nearby islands. I also had the pleasure of trying some delicious seafood at a local restaurant.

I had an amazing time in Bulgaria, and I would highly recommend it to anyone looking for a unique and unforgettable travel experience.

Made in the USA
Las Vegas, NV
03 January 2024

83883536R00069